She Believed!

A Journal

ROGENA MITCHELL-JONES MANUSCRIPT SERVICE

ROGENA MITCHELL-JONES MANUSCRIPT SERVICE
ROGENA MITCHELL-JONES JOURNALS
WWW.ROGENAMITCHELL.COM

COLLEGE RULE EDITION 2017

ISBN-13: 978-1540885302
ISBN-10: 1540885305

MAKE EACH DAY A *Masterpiece*

She believed she could so she did.

She believed she could so she did.

She believed she could so she did.

She believed she could so she did.

She believed she could so she did.

She believed she could so she did.

She believed she could so she did.

She believed she could so she did.

She believed she could so she did.

She believed she could so she did.

She believed she could so she did.

She believed she could so she did.

She believed she could so she did.

She believed she could so she did.

She believed she could so she did.

She believed she could so she did.

She believed she could so she did.

She believed she could so she did.

She believed she could so she did.

She believed she could so she did.

She believed she could so she did.

She believed she could so she did.

She believed she could so she did.

She believed she could so she did.

She believed she could so she did.

She believed she could so she did.

She believed she could so she did.

She believed she could so she did.

She believed she could so she did.

She believed she could so she did.

She believed she could so she did.

She believed she could so she did.

She believed she could so she did.

She believed she could so she did.

She believed she could so she did.

She believed she could so she did.

She believed she could so she did.

She believed she could so she did.

She believed she could so she did.

She believed she could so she did.

She believed she could so she did.

She believed she could so she did.

She believed she could so she did.

She believed she could so she did.

She believed she could so she did.

She believed she could so she did.

She believed she could so she did.

She believed she could so she did.

She believed she could so she did.

She believed she could so she did.

She believed she could so she did.

She believed she could so she did.

She believed she could so she did.

She believed she could so she did.

She believed she could so she did.

She believed she could so she did.

She believed she could so she did.

She believed she could so she did.

She believed she could so she did.

She believed she could so she did.

She believed she could so she did.

She believed she could so she did.

She believed she could so she did.

She believed she could so she did.

She believed she could so she did.

She believed she could so she did.

She believed she could so she did.

She believed she could so she did.

She believed she could so she did.

She believed she could so she did.

She believed she could so she did.

She believed she could so she did.

She believed she could so she did.

She believed she could so she did.

She believed she could so she did.

She believed she could so she did.

She believed she could so she did.

She believed she could so she did.

She believed she could so she did.

She believed she could so she did.

She believed she could so she did.

She believed she could so she did.

She believed she could so she did.

She believed she could so she did.

She believed she could so she did.

She believed she could so she did.

She believed she could so she did,

She believed she could so she did.

She believed she could so she did.

She believed she could so she did.

She believed she could so she did.

She believed she could so she did.

TO ORDER ADDITIONAL JOURNALS, GO TO
AMAZON OR THE CREATESPACE ONLINE STORE.
SEARCH ROGENA MITCHELL-JONES JOURNALS.

OR DIRECT FROM THE AUTHOR AT
ROGENA@ROGENAMITCHELL.COM

RMJ MANUSCRIPT SERVICE
WWW.ROGENAMITCHELL.COM

"Proficient in grammar, and brilliant in the knowledge that authenticates writing, is one of the top editors in the country for a reason. She is that good! Her encyclop mind delves into finding meanings. She sorts all the components it takes to make b come alive with realism."

—KIERAN YORK, BESTSELLING AUTHOR &

AUTHOR OF APPOINTMENT WITH A SMILE, NIGHT WITHOUT

AND LITERARY FICTION AT ITS BEST—TOURING KELLY'S POEM—JUST TO NAME A

* * * * *

"On the shore, there was a voice of reason. It was a voice who spoke of telling a st not about gerunds and gerundives. It spoke of the power of words strung together, only to convey a concept, but also to tell a story, to draw forth from the reader their told, unrealized story. And the voice was Rogena Mitchell-Jones."

—BAER CHARLTON, AUTHOR OF THE PULITZER PRIZE NOMINATED

STONEHEART: A PATH OF IDENTITY AND REDEM

RMJ MANUSCRIPT SERVICE

A PROFESSIONAL EDITING SERVICE | FREELANCE EDITING WITH AFFORDABLE RATES

STRIVING FOR EXCELLENCE FOR YOU, THE AUTHOR, PROVIDING CONCISE LITERARY & TECHNICAL EDITING.

Currently, Rogena Mitchell-Jones lives in South Jersey with her wife, Karen, and their extremely pampered cats. If she isn't at home editing or reading, you might find her on the beach—book in hand.

Her background consists of over 25 years in journalism and now editing full time for independent authors internationally since 2013. Her clientele base includes a vast array of Amazon, USA Today, and NY Times Best Selling Authors.

The end of 2014, Rogena was nominated as best editor in an awards event sponsored by The Kindle Hub—TKH Book Awards 2014. With nearly sixty editors competing, she advanced to the finals and came in second in the final competition. With the title of BEST EDITOR 2014 Finalist, it shows hard work does pay off.

She isn't a writer—She's an editor. She is here because she wants to assist you, the author, in creating a manuscript free of typographical errors, including misspelled words, grammatical errors, and inconsistencies in plot and characters.

She gives attention to detail. With this attention to detail, she is able to polish your future best seller, like polishing fine silver that once belonged to your grandmother. Let's make your manuscript the masterpiece you have dreamed of publishing.

She is an editor, not an author. She is a reader, not a writer. She is a Copy Editor. She wants to live in your story while reading your manuscript.

She is here to assist you so you will have a result allowing your future readers to enjoy your published work.

Contact her on Facebook or via email at rogena@rogenamitchell.com.

ROGENA MITCHELL-JONES MANUSCRIPT SERVICE
WWW.ROGENAMITCHELL.COM

Made in the USA
Columbia, SC
21 May 2018